STRUM & SING

Lyrics, chord symbols and guitar chord diagrams for 20 songs

BOB MARLEY

Contents

ISBN 978-1-5400-5776-1

Cover image © Getty Images / Rob Verhorst / Contributor

HAL•LEONARD®

Visit Hal Leonard Online at
www.halleonard.com

World headquarters, contact:
Hal Leonard
7777 West Bluemound Road
Milwaukee, WI 53213
Email: info@halleonard.com

In Europe, contact:
Hal Leonard Europe Limited
42 Wigmore Street
Marylebone, London, W1U 2RN
Email: info@halleonardeurope.com

In Australia, contact:
Hal Leonard Australia Pty. Ltd.
4 Lentara Court
Cheltenham, Victoria, 3192 Australia
Email: info@halleonard.com.au

from *Natural Mystic*

Africa Unite

Words and Music by Bob Marley

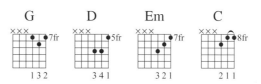

Intro

|**G**   **D**   **Em** |

G   **D**   **Em** |
Stay up, oh, yah, yop, bob, by-up, ah.

G   **D**   **Em** |
Deedle, ee, dup, boop, oop, oodle, ooh.

G   **D**   **Em**   ‖
Steh-dup, eh, da, da, mm, da, dep, eh.

Chorus 1

G   **D**   **Em**
  Afri - ca unite,

            |**C**   **D**   **Em**
'Cause we're moving right out of Bab - ylon

         |**C**   **D**   **Em** | ‖
And we're going to our fath - er's land, yah.

Verse 1

G   **D** |**Em**
  How good and how pleasant it would be

            C |**G**
Before God and man, yeah,

            D |**Em**   **C** |**G**
To see the u - nification of all   Afri - cans, yay.

            D |**Em**
As it's been said already,

         C |**G**
"Let it be done," yeah.

            D |**Em**
We are the children of the

      C |**G**
Rasta - man.

            D |**Em**
We are the children of the

      C   ‖
Higher man, whoa.

Chorus 2

G   D   Em
  Afri - ca unite,

     |G   D   Em
'Cause the children wanna go home.

                |G
Yeah, yeah, yeah.

      D   Em
Afri - ca unite,

        |C   D   Em
'Cause we're moving right out of Bab - ylon

        |C   D   Em |
And we're grooving to our fath - er's land.

              ‖
Yay.

Verse 2

G   D |Em
  How good and how pleasant it would be

      C |G
Before God and man

         D |Em
To see the u - nification of all

      C |G
Rasta - man, hey.

      D |Em
As it's been said already,

      C |G
"Let it be done," mm.

      D |Em
I'll tell you who we are

      C |G
Under the sun,

      D |Em
We are the children of the

      C |G
Rasta - man.

      D |Em
We are the children of the

      C   ‖
Higher man, so...

Outro

```
     G       D      Em    |
   Afri - ca unite,

 G           D      Em
Afri, Afri - ca unite, yeah.
    |G           D           Em
U - nite for the benefit of your people.
    |G           D           Em
U - nite, for it's later than you think.
    |G           D           Em
U - nite for the benefit of your children.
    |G           D           Em
U - nite, for it's later than you think.
       |G       D       Em
Af - rica a - wait its creators.
          |G       D        Em
Afri - ca, a - waiting its creators.
          |G           D           Em                    ‖
Af - rica, you're my forefath - er's cornerstone, unite.
```

Buffalo Soldier

Words and Music by Noel Williams and Bob Marley

A   F#m   D   C#m   A/C#   E/B   E

Intro |A | | | ‖

Verse 1

A
Buffalo soldier,
F#m |A
Dreadlock Rasta.

It was a buffalo soldier
|F#m |A
In the heart of America.

Stolen from Africa,
F#m |A
Brought to America.

Fighting on arrival,
F#m |A   ‖
Fighting for survival.

Chorus 1

D   C#m |D   C#m |A/C#
    If you know your hist - ory,
                E/B |F#m |D
Then you would know where you're coming from.
            C#m |D   C#m |A/C#
Then you wouldn't have to ask me
            E/B |F#m
Who the heck do I think I am.

Verse 2

    ‖A |
I'm just the buffalo soldier
  |F♯m |A |
In the heart of America.

     | |
Stolen from Africa,
F♯m |A
Brought to America.

     | | |
Said, he was fighting on arrival,
F♯m |A
Fighting for survival.

      | |
Said, he was the buffalo soldier
  |F♯m |A
In the war for America.

    ‖
Tell ya.

Interlude

‖:A
 Why, yi, yi?

  | |
Why, yi, yi, yi?
F♯m |A   :‖
Why, yi, yi, yi, yi, yi, yi, yi?

Bridge

F♯m |
Buffalo soldier,
    |D |C♯m
Trod into the land, whoa.
     |F♯m |
Said, he would've ran and make you wanna hang,
    |D
Trod into the land,
 |C♯m
Yes.

Verse 3

```
        E        ‖A              |
Said he was a buffalo soldier
        |F♯m            |A                |
In the war for America.

                   |              |
Buffalo soldier,
F♯m            |A              |
Dreadlock Rasta.

                   |              |
Fighting on arrival,
F♯m                |A              |
Fighting for survival.

                            |
Driven from the mainland
        |F♯m                    |A
To the heart of the Caribbean.
                   ‖
Singin'...
```

Outro

```
‖:A
  Why, yi, yi?
   |              |
Why, yi, yi, yi?
F♯m            |A                    :‖ Repeat and fade
Why, yi, yi, yi, yi, yi, yi, yi?
```

Could You Be Loved

Words and Music by Bob Marley

Intro

|Bm | | |
| | | ‖

Chorus 1

D　　　　　|Bm　　　　|G
　Could you be loved?
　　　|D　　　|
Then be loved.
　　　　　|Bm　　　　|G
Could you be loved?
　　|D　　　‖
Then be loved.

Verse 1

Bm　　　　|　　　　　|Em　　　　|　　　　|Bm
　　Don't let them fool ya
　　　　　|　　　|Em
Or even try to school ya.
　　　|　　　|Bm
Oh, no.
　　　|
We've got a mind of our own.
　　|G　　　F#m
So, go to hell if what
　　　　|Em*　　|Bm
You thinkin' is not right.
　　　　　|
Love would nev - er leave us alone.
　|G
Ah, in the darkness,
　　F#m　　　|A　　　　‖
There must come out to light.

Chorus 2

D |Bm |G
 Could you be loved?

    |D |
Then be loved.

       |Bm
Now, could you be loved?

 |G
Whoa, yeah.

    |D |Bm   ‖
Then be loved.

Bridge

Bm | |
Could you be loved, now, could you be loved?

  | |
The road of life is rocky and you may stumble, too.

 |
So, why don't you point your fingers

    | |
At someone else that's judging you?

            |
(Could you be, could you be, could you be loved?

       |
Could you be, could you be loved?

          |
Could you be, could you be, could you be loved?

       ‖
Could you be, could you be loved?)

Verse 2

Bm | | |Em | |Bm

    Don't let them change ya, oh,

| |Em

Or even rear - range ya.

| |Bm

Oh, no.

| |

We've got the life to live.

  G   F♯m |Em*

(Oo, oo,   oo.)

|Bm

They say

|

Only, only,

  |G   F♯m |A | |

Only the fittest of the fittest shall survive.

‖

Stay alive, eh.

Chorus 3

D |Bm |G

    Could you be loved?

|D |

Then be loved.

|Bm

Now, could you be loved?

|G |D ‖

Whoa, yeah, then be loved.

Outro

Bm |

(Ain't gonna miss the water un - til the well runs dry.

| | |

And no matter how you treat the man, he'll never be satisfied.)

‖: | :‖ *Repeat and fade*

Say something, say something.

from *One Love: The Very Best of Bob Marley and the Wailers*

Get Up Stand Up

Words and Music by Bob Marley and Peter Tosh

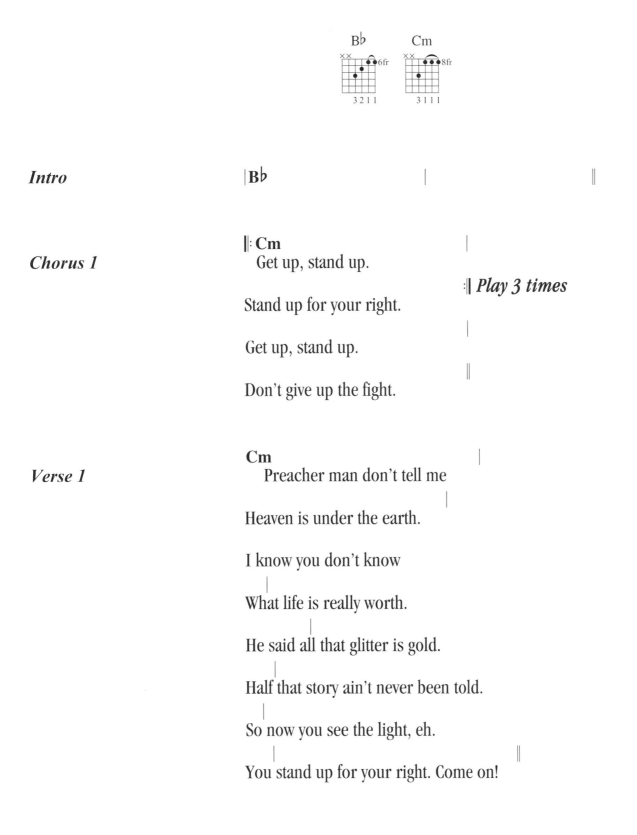

Intro |B♭ | ‖

Chorus 1 ‖: **Cm** |

Get up, stand up.

Stand up for your right.   :‖ *Play 3 times*

Get up, stand up. |

Don't give up the fight.   ‖

Verse 1 **Cm** |

Preacher man don't tell me |

Heaven is under the earth.

I know you don't know |

What life is really worth. |

He said all that glitter is gold. |

Half that story ain't never been told. |

So now you see the light, eh. |

You stand up for your right. Come on!   ‖

Chorus 2

‖: **Cm** |

  Get up, stand up.

|

Stand up for your right.

|

Get up, stand up.

:‖

Don't give up the fight.

Verse 2

Cm

  Most people think

| |

Great God will come from the sky,

Take away everything

| |

And make everybody feel high.

|

But if you know what life is worth

You would look for yours on earth.

|

And now a you see the light.

| ‖

You stand up for your right. Jah!

Chorus 3

 Cm |

(Get up, stand up.) Jah. Jah.

|

(Stand up for your right.) Oh, hoo.

|

(Get up, stand up.) Get up, stand up.

|

(Don't give up the fight.) Life is your right.

|

(Get up, stand up.) So, we can't give up the fight.

|

(Stand up for your right.) Lord, Lord.

|

(Get up, stand up.) Keep us loving on.

(Don't give up the fight.) Yeah.

Verse 3

‖**Cm** |

We're sick and tired of your ism schism game,

|

Dyin' and go to heaven in a Jesus' name, Lord.

|

We know and we understand

Almighty God is a living man.

|

You can fool some people sometimes,

|

But you can't fool all the people all the time.

|

So now we see the light,

|

We gonna stand up for our rights.

‖

So, you better...

Outro-Chorus

‖: **Cm** |

Get up, stand up.

|

Stand up for your right.

|

Get up, stand up.

:‖ *Repeat and fade*
w/ lead vocal ad lib.

Don't give up the fight.

Exodus

Words and Music by Bob Marley

Am

Intro

|**Am** | |

Exodus.

Movement of Jah peo - ple.

Oh, yeah. Open your eyes and let me tell you this.

Verse 1

Am

Men and people will fight you down. Tell me why.

(When you see Jah light.) Ha, ha, ha, ha, ha, ha!

Let me tell you if you're not wrong, then why? (Well, everything is alright.)

So we're gonna walk, alright, through the roads of creation.

We, the generation, tell me why, (Trod through great tribulation.)

Trod through great tribulation.

Chorus 1

Am

Exodus, alright.

Movement of Jah peo - ple.

Oh, yeah, oh, yeah,

Alright.

Exodus.

Movement of Jah peo - ple.

Oh, yeah.

Yeah, yeah, yeah, well.

Verse 2

Am

Uh, open your eyes.   (Look within.)

Are you satisfied? (With the life you're living?) Huh.

We know where we're going, uh, we know where we're from.

We leavin' Babylon, we're going to our fatherland, two, three, four.

Chorus 2

Am

Exodus.

Movement of Jah peo - ple. Oh, yeah.

(Movement of Jah people.)

Send us another brother Moses,

From across the Red Sea.

Send us another brother Moses,

From across the Red Sea.

Interlude

‖: Am   :‖ *Play 3 times*
    Move!   *Move!*

Verse 3

Am

Open your eyes and look within.

Are you satisfied with the life you're living?

We know where we're going, we know where we're from.

                                                    N.C.   ‖
We leavin' Babylon, yah, we're going to our father's land.

Chorus 3

Am

Exodus. Alright, alright.

Movement of Jah peo - ple.

Oh, yeah.

Exodus.

Movement of Jah peo - ple.

Outro

‖: Am   :‖
    Move!   *Move!*

‖:   :‖ *Repeat and fade*
    (Movement of Jah people.)

I Shot the Sheriff

Words and Music by Bob Marley

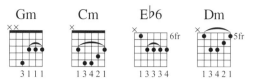

Chorus 1

Gm   **|Cm**
(I shot the sheriff,

                |Gm
But I didn't shoot no deputy.

      | |
Oh, no, oh.

          |Cm
I shot the sheriff,

                |Gm
But I didn't shoot no deputy.

      | ‖
Oo, oo, oo.) Yeah.

Verse 1

E♭6 **Dm**   **|Gm**
  All a - round in my hometown,

      |E♭6 **Dm**   **|Gm**
They try - in' to track me down,   yeah.

     |E♭6   **Dm**   **|Gm**
They say they want to bring me in guilty

     |E♭6   **Dm** **|Gm**
For the killing of a depu - ty,

     |E♭6 **Dm** **|Gm**
For the life of a depu - ty.

        | |
But I say.

          | ‖
Oh now, now, oh.

Chorus 2

Gm |Cm
(I shot the sheriff,) The sher - iff.

       |Gm
(But I swear it was in self-defense.)

      |
Lord knows. (Oo, oo, oo.)

    | |Cm
Yeah, I said, I shot the sheriff. Oh, Lord.

      |Gm
(And they say it is a capital offense.

  | ‖
Oo, oo, oo.)

Verse 2

E♭6 Dm |Gm
 Sheriff John Brown always hated me.

|E♭6 Dm |Gm
For what, I don't know.

  |E♭6 Dm |Gm
Every - time I plant a seed,

  |E♭6   Dm |Gm
He said kill it be - fore it grow.

  |E♭6   Dm |Gm |
He said kill them be - fore they grow and so,

     | |
And so,

     ‖
Read it in the news.

Chorus 3

    Gm   **|Cm**
(I shot the sheriff,) Lord.

                   |Gm
(But I swear it was in self-defense.)

                    |
Where was the deputy?

    | **|Cm**
I said, I shot the sheriff,

               |Gm
But I swear it was in self-defense.

       | **‖**
Yeah. (Oo.)

Verse 3

E♭6   **Dm**   **|Gm**
  Freedom came my way one day

    |E♭6   **Dm**   **|Gm**   **|E♭6**
And I started out of town, yeah.

             Dm   **|Gm**
All of the sud - den, I saw Sheriff John Brown

   |E♭6 **Dm**   **|Gm**
Aimin' to shoot me down.

    |E♭6   **Dm**
So I shot, I shot,

      |Gm   **|**   **|**
I shot him down and I say

     | **|**   **‖**
If I am guilty, I will pay.

Chorus 4

   Gm   **|Cm**
(I shot the sheriff,) But, I say.

                    |Gm
(But I didn't shoot no deputy.)

                  | **|**
I didn't shoot no depu - ty, no.

                |Cm
(I shot the sheriff,

                |Gm
But I didn't shoot no deputy.)

             |
Oh. (Oo, oo, oo.) Yeah.

Verse 4

   ‖E♭6   **Dm**   **|Gm**
Re - flexes had the better of me

 |E♭6   **Dm**   **|Gm**
And what is to be must be.

      |E♭6 Dm   **|Gm**   **|**
Every - day the bucket a-go-a well.

E♭6   **Dm**   **|Gm**   **|**
One day, the bottom a-go drop out.

E♭6   **Dm**   **|Gm**   **|**
One day, the bottom a-go drop out.

        | **|**   **|**
I say.

Chorus 5

  ‖Gm   **|Cm**
I, I, I,   I shot the sheriff,

                        |Gm   **|**
Lord, I didn't shoot the deputy, no.

        | **|Cm**
Yeah, I, I... (Shot the sher - iff.)

                 |Gm   **|**
But I didn't shoot no deputy.

            ‖
Yeah, no, yeah.

from *One Love: The Very Best of Bob Marley and the Wailers*

Iron Lion Zion

Words and Music by Bob Marley

F#m   E   D6   Bm   A   D   Em   Bm*   A*

Intro

|F#m E D6 | Bm A Bm |D |Em |

|D |Em |D |Em |

|D |Em |

Verse 1

‖**Bm*** | **Em**
Yeah, I'm on the rock

|**Bm*** | **Em**
And then I check a stock.

|**Bm*** | **Em**
I had to run like a fugitive

|**Bm*** |
To save the life I live.

Chorus 1

Em   ‖**D**
I'm gonna be iron

|**A***
Like a lion

|**Bm*** |
In Zion.

|**D**
I'm gonna be iron

|**A***
Like a lion

|**Bm***
In Zion.

|**F#m E D6** | **Bm A Bm** |

F#m E D6 | **Bm   A   Bm** ‖
Iron, lion, Zion.   (Lion.)

Verse 2

  Bm* | **Em**
I'm on the run,
    |**Bm*** | **Em**
But I ain't got no gun.
     |**Bm*** | **Em**
See, they want to be the star,
     |**Bm*** |
So they fighting tribal war.
  Em   ‖
And they saying...

Chorus 2

  D
Iron
    |**A***
Like a lion
   |**Bm*** | |
In Zion.
  D
Iron
    |**A***
Like a lion
   |**Bm***
In Zion.
|**F♯m E D6** | **Bm A Bm** |

F♯m E **D6** | **Bm** **A**   **Bm** ‖
Iron, lion, Zion.   (Lion.)

Sax Solo

|**D** |**Em** |**D** |**Em** |
|**D** |**Em** |**D** |**Em**

Verse 3

   ‖**Bm*** | **Em** |
Yeah, I'm on the rock.
Bm* | **Em**
(Runnin', and you're runnin'.)
    |**Bm*** | **Em** |
See you pop, I take a stock.
Bm* | **Em**
(Runnin' like a fugitive.)
    |**Bm*** | **Em** |**Bm**
I had to run like a fugitive,
       | **Em**
Oo, God,
    |**Bm*** | **Em** |**Bm***
Just to, just to save the life I live.
     |
Oh, now,

Chorus 3

    Em   ‖**D**
I'm gonna be iron

    |**A***
Like a lion

 |**Bm*** |
In Zion.

       |**D**
I'm gonna be iron

    |**A***
Like a lion

 |**Bm***
In Zion.

|**F♯m E D6** | **Bm A Bm** |

F♯m E D6 | **Bm A Bm** |
Iron, lion, Zion.
F♯m E D6 | **Bm A Bm** |
Iron, lion, Zion.
F♯m E D6 | **Bm A Bm** ‖
Iron, lion, Zion.   (Lion.)

Outro

‖:**D**
 Iron

    |**A***
Like a lion

 |**Bm*** | :‖ *Repeat and fade*
In Zion.

Is This Love

Words and Music by Bob Marley

Intro

|F#m | |D |A |

|F#m | |D |A

Verse 1

E ‖F#m |D

I wanna love ya

|A

And treat you right.

E |F#m |

I wanna love ya

|D |A

Every day and every night.

E |F#m |

We'll be togeth - er

|D |A

With a roof right over our heads.

E |F#m | |

We'll share the shel - ter

D |A

Of my single bed.

E |F#m |

We'll share the same room, yeah.

|D |A

Oh, Jah provide our bread.

Chorus 1

‖C#m |

Is this love, is this love, is this love

|Bm |

Is this love that I'm feeling?

|C#m |

Is this love, is this love, is this love,

|Bm | |

Is this love that I'm feeling?

| C#m D* |E* ‖

Bridge 1

```
    D                           |
     I wanna know, wanna know,
                        |Bm   C♯m   D* |E*  D*  C♯m |
    Wanna know, now.

                                |
    I've got to know, got to know,

                                |
    Got to know, now.

        |                   |Bm          |
    I, ___ I'm willing and a - ble.
      |F♯m*          |                  | E*  D* |C♯m   Bm
    So I      throw my cards on your ta - ble.
```

Verse 2

```
            ‖F♯m           |D
    I wanna love ya. I wanna
                    |A      E          |F♯m
    Love and treat, love and treat you right.
                    |
    I wanna love ya

        |D              |A
    Every day and every night.
        E         |F♯m         |
    We'll be togeth - er, yeah,
            |D                    |A
    With a roof right over our heads.
        E              |F♯m         |
    We'll share the shel - ter, yeah,
            |D               |A
    Oh, yeah, of my single bed.
        E            |F♯m            |
    We'll share the same room, yeah.
        |D                    |A
    Oh, Jah provides the bread.
```

Chorus 2

```
            ‖C♯m                  |
    Is this love, is this love, is this love
                        |Bm          |
    Is this love that I'm feeling?
        |C♯m                   |
    Is this love, is this love, is this love,
                        |Bm          |
    Is this love that I'm feeling?
            |        C♯m   D* |E*           ‖
    Whoa.
```

Bridge 2

    D
   Oh, yes, I know, yes,

| |Bm C#m   D* |E* D* C#m |
I know, yes, I know now.

Oh, yes, I know, yes,

 | |
I know, yes, I know now.

   | |Bm |
I, ___ I'm willing and a - ble,
  |F#m* | |E*   D* |C#m
So I   throw my cards on your ta - ble.

Outro-Verse

      Bm   ‖F#m
See, I wanna love ya.
      |D |A
I wanna love and treat ya,
      E |F#m
Love and treat you right.
     | |D
I wanna love ya every day
         |A
And every night.
    E |F#m |
We'll be together
     |D |A
With a roof right over our heads.
    E |F#m | |
We'll share the shel - ter
D |A
Of my single bed.
    E |F#m | |
We'll share the same room, yeah.
D |A
Jah provides the bread.
    E |F#m | |
We'll share the shel - ter
D |A   ‖
Of my single bed.

Jamming

Words and Music by Bob Marley

Intro

|Bm |E7 |G |F#m

|

Oo, yeah.

|Bm |E7 |G |F#m

Chorus 1

‖Bm |E7 |G

Alright, we're jamming.

    |F#m

I wanna jam it with you.

  |Bm

We're jamming,

  |E7

Jam - ming

  |G |F#m

And I hope you like jamming, too.

Verse 1

‖Bm   E7

Ain't no rules, ain't no vow,

   |Bm   E7 |

We can do it anyhow.

G |F#m

I and I will see you through,

   |Bm   E7

'Cause every - day we pay the price.

  |Bm   E7 |

We are the living sacri - fice,

G |F#m

Jamming 'til the jam is through.

Chorus 2

‖**Bm** |**E7**
We're jamming.

|**G** |**F♯m**
To think that jamming was a thing of the past.

|**Bm** |**E7**
We're jamming.

|**G** |**F♯m**
And I hope this jam is gonna last.

Verse 2

‖**Bm** **E7**
No bullets could stop us now,

|**Bm** **E7** |
We neither beg, nor we won't bow.

G |**F♯m**
Neither can be bought nor sold.

|**Bm** **E7**
We all defend the right,

|**Bm** **E7**
Jah Jah children must u - nite.

|**G** |**F♯m**
Well, life is worth much more than gold.

Chorus 3

‖**Bm** |**E7**
We're jamming, (Jamming, jamming, jamming.)

|**G** |**F♯m**
And we're jamming in the name of the Lord.

|**Bm** |**E7**
We're jamming, (Jamming, jamming.) look out. (Jamming.)

|**G** |**F♯m** ‖
We're jamming right straight from yard. Singin'...

Interlude

Bm |**Em** |**Bm**
Holy Mount Zion,

|**Em** |**Bm** **N.C.**
Holy Mount Zion.

| |**Bm** **N.C.**
Jah sitteth in Mount Zion

|
And rules all creation.

Chorus 4

‖**Bm**
Yeah, we're,

|**E7**
We're jamming,

(Bop, chu, wah.)

|**Bm**
Bop, chu, wah, wah, wah.

|**E7**
We're jamming,

|**G**
(Bop, chu, wah.) see,

|**F♯m**
I want to jam it with you.

|**Bm** |**E7**
We're jamming, (Jamming, jamming, jamming.)

|**G** |**F♯m**
And, jam down, hope you're jamming, too.

Verse 3

‖**Bm**   **E7**
Jah knows how much I've tried.

|**Bm**   **E7** |**G**
The truth I cannot hide

|**F♯m**
To keep you satisfied.

|**Bm**   **E7**
True love that I know ex - ists

|**Bm**   **E7** |**G**
Is the love I can't resist, so

|**F♯m**
Jam by my side.

Outro-Chorus

||Bm |E7 |G

We're jamming. (Jamming, jamming, jamming.)

       |F#m

I want to jam it with you.

   |Bm

We're jamming, we're jamming, we're jamming, we're jamming.

   |E7 |

We're jamming, we're jamming, we're jamming, we're jamming.

G |F#m

Hope you like jamming, too.

   |Bm

We're jamming, we're jamming. (Jamming.)

   |E7 |G

We're jamming, we're jamming. (Jamming.)

     |F#m

I want, I want, I want to jam with you, now.

   |Bm |E7 |G |F#m

We're jamming, we're jamming. (Hope you like jamming, too.)

    |Bm

Hey, and I hope you like jamming.

 |E7 |G

I hope you like jamming 'cause (I want to jam it with you.)

 |F#m |Bm |E7

I want to jam it with you.

      |G

I like, I hope you,

 |F#m |Bm |E7

I hope you like a-jamming, too.

      |G |F#m

I want to jam it,

     |Bm

Want to jam it.

    |E7 |G |Bm ||

Oo, hoo.

from *One Love: The Very Best of Bob Marley and the Wailers*

Lively Up Yourself

Words and Music by Bob Marley

```
      D              G
   xx              x       x
        10fr              10fr
   3 2 1 1         1 3 3 3
```

Intro

|D |G |D
   Woo, hoo!

|G |D
Oh!

      |G
Oh, yeah.

|D |G
Oh, yeah.

Chorus 1

     ‖D |G
You're gonna lively up yourself

       |D |G
And don't be no drag.

|D |G
You lively up yourself,

     |D |G
Oh, reggae is a - nother bag.

|D |G
You lively up yourself

     |D |G
And don't say no.

    |D |G
You're gonna lively up yourself

    |D
'Cause I said so.

|G
Hear what you gonna do.

Verse 1

‖**D** |**G**
You rock so, you rock so,

|**D** |**G**
Like you never did before, yeah.

|**D** |**G**
You dip so, you dip so,

|**D** |**G**
Dip through my door.

|**D** |**G**
You come so, you come so.

|**D** |**G**
Oh, yeah.

|**D** |**G**
You skank so, you skank so,

|**D** |**G**
Be alive to - day.

Chorus 2

‖**D** |**G**
You're gonna lively up yourself,

|**D** |**G**
And don't say no.

|**D** |**G**
You lively up yourself,

|**D** |**G**
Big daddy says so, y'all.

|**D** |**G**
You lively up yourself,

|**D** |**G**
And don't be no drag.

|**D** |**G**
You lively up yourself,

|**D** |**G** ‖
'Cause reggae is a - nother bag.

Verse 2

D |G
  What you got

             |D |G |D
That I don't know?

             |G
I'm a - tryin' to won - der, wonder,

     |D |G
Won - der, why you wonder,

              |D |G ||
Wonder why you act so, act so.

Interlude 1

D |G |D |G |D
  Yeah.

               |G ||
Hey, did you hear what the man said?

Chorus 3

D |G
Lively up your,

             |D |G
Your woman in the morning time, y'all.

  |D |
Ah! Keep a - lively up your woman

G
When the evening come

     |D |G ||
And take you, take you, take you, take you.

Interlude 2

D |G
  Come on, baby, 'cause I,

    |D |G |
I wanna be lively myself, y'all.

||: D |G |D |G   :|| *Play 7 times*

Chorus 4

```
D            |G          |D          |G          |
Lively up yourself.
D            |G          |D          |G
Lively up yourself.
```

Sax Solo

```
            ‖D                    |G          |
You're gonna rock, so you rock, so.
‖:D              |G                  :‖ Play 7 times
```

Verse 3

```
            ‖D              |G            |D            |G
You rock so, you rock so.
            |D              |G            |D            |G
You dip so, you dip so.
            |D                    |G
You skank so, you skank so,
                         |D                  |G
And don't be no drag.
            |D                    |G
You come so, you come so.
                         |D                  |G
Oh, reggae is a - nother bag.
                                   |D                  |G                      ‖
Get what you got in that bag.
```

Outro

```
D                                          |
    Oh, what you got, did you have a bag
G                    |D            |G            |D
You got hangin' there?
                         |G            |D
What you say you got?
      |G              |D              |G            |
I don't believe you.
|D              |G            ‖
```

Natural Mystic

Words and Music by Bob Marley

Am   Dm   G

Intro

‖: Am   :‖ *Play 3 times*

Verse 1

‖**Dm**   **G** |**Am**
There's a natural mystic blowing through the air.

|**Dm**   **G** |**Am**
If you listen carefully, now, you will hear,

|**Dm**   **Am**
This could be the first trum - pet,

|**Dm**   **Am**
Might as well be the last.

|**Dm**   **Am**
Man - y more will have to suf - fer,

|**Dm**   **G**   **Am**
Man - y more will have to die,

Dm |**Am**   ‖
Don't ask me why.

Verse 2

Dm   **G** |**Am**
Things are not the way they used to be,

|
I won't tell no lie.

|**Dm**   **G** |**Am**
One and all gotta face reality, now.

|**Dm**   **Am**
Though I try to find the answer

|**Dm**   **Am**
To all the questions they ask,

|**Dm**   **Am**
Though I know it's impos - sible

|**Dm**   **G**   **Am**
To go living through the past.

Dm |**Am**
Don't tell no lie.

Chorus 1

   ‖Dm   G |Am   Dm

There's a natural mystic blowing through the air,

               |Am

Can't keep them down.

 |Dm   G |Am

If you listen carefully, now, you will hear

That's a natural mystic

Blowing through the air.

Verse 3

   ‖Dm   Am

This could be the first trum - pet,

   |Dm   Am

Might as well be the last.

   |Dm   Am

Man - y more will have to suf - fer,

   |Dm   G   Am

Man - y more will have to die,

  Dm |Am

Don't ask me why.

   |Dm   G |Am

There's a natural mystic blowing through the air,

I won't tell no lie.

 |Dm   G |Am

If you listen careful - ly, now, you will hear.

Outro-Chorus

   ‖Dm   G |Am

There's a natural mystic blowing through the air,

Such a natural mystic blowing through the air.

There's a natural mystic blowing through the air,

Such a natural mystic blowing through the air.

Such a natural mystic blowing through the air.

No Woman No Cry

Words and Music by Bob Marley

C   Cadd2/B   Am   F   G

Intro

|C   Cadd2/B |Am   F |C F C| G ||

Chorus 1

C Cadd2/B |Am   F |
No, woman, no cry.

C F   C| G |
No, woman, no cry.

C Cadd2/B |Am   F |
No, woman, no cry.

C F   C| G
No, woman, no cry.

||
'Cause, 'cause,

Verse 1

C   Cadd2/B |Am   F |C
  'Cause I re - member a - when we used to sit

       Cadd2/B |Am   F |C
In a govern - ment yard in Trenchtown.

     Cadd2/B |Am   F |C
Oba, oba - serving the hyp - ocrites,   yeah,

       Cadd2/B |Am   F |C
Mingle with the good people we meet,   yeah,

       Cadd2/B |
Good-a friends we have, oh,

Am   F |C
Good friends we have lost

  Cadd2/B |Am F |C
A - long the way, ____ yeah.)

      Cadd2/B|Am   F |C
In this bright future, you can't forget your past.

     Cadd2/B |Am F ||
So dry your tears, I say,   yeah.

Chorus 2

```
                 C   Cadd2/B   |Am    F     |
                 No, woman, no cry.
                 C    F        C|          G        |C
                 No, woman, no cry,        hey, yeah.
                              Cadd2/B    |
                 Ah, little darlin',
                 Am            F      |C
                 Don't shed no tears.
                     F          C|
                 No, woman, no cry,
                    G              ‖
                 Yeah, say, say.
```

Verse 2

```
                 C            Cadd2/B  |Am              F         |C
                    Said I re - member a - when we use to sit
                             Cadd2/B        |Am     F          |C
                 In the govern - ment's yard in Trenchtown,      yeah.
                              Cadd2/B        |Am     F       |C
                 And then Georg - ie would make the fire light, I say,
                             Cadd2/B          |Am      F     |C
                 A - log - a - wood - a burning - a through the nights,      yeah.
                             Cadd2/B    |Am          F        |C
                 Then we would cook cornmeal porridge,       I say,
                         Cadd2/B   |Am      F        |C
                 Of which I'll share with you, _____   yeah.
                     Cadd2/B   |Am        F           |C
                 My feet is my on - ly carriage,       and so,
                        Cadd2/B       |Am
                 I've got to push on through.
                            F          ‖
                 But while I'm gone...
```

Bridge

```
             C                 Cadd2/B      |Am
             Everything is gonna be alright.
                               F      |C
             Everything's gonna be alright.
                               Cadd2/B      |Am
             Everything's gonna be alright.
                               F      |C
             Everything's gonna be alright.
                               Cadd2/B      |Am
             Everything's gonna be alright, yeah.
                               F      |C
             Everything's gonna be alright.
                               Cadd2/B      |Am
             Everything's gonna be alright, yeah.
                               F
             Everything's gonna be alright.
```

Chorus 3

```
             ‖C   Cadd2/B  |Am   F    |
             So, no, woman, no cry.
             C   F         C|       G    |C
             No, woman, no cry,       I say.
                     Cadd2/B     |Am
             Oh little, oh little darling,
                           F          |C
             Don't shed no tears.
                     F          C|           G    |C
             No, woman, no cry,         yay.
                     Cadd2/B|Am
             No, woman, no, woman,
                     F            |C
             No, woman, no cry.
                     F          C|
             No, woman, no cry.
                              G          |C
             One more time, I've got to say.
                     Cadd2/B        |
             Oh, little, little darling,
             Am               F         |C
             Please don't shed no tears.
                     F          C|        G    ‖
             No, woman, no cry.
```

Outro-Guitar Solo   ‖: C   Cadd2/B |Am   F |C   F   C| G   :‖ *Play 4 times*

One Love/People Get Ready

One Love
Words and Music by Bob Marley
People Get Ready
Words and Music by Curtis Mayfield

B♭	F	E♭	Gm
×××　6fr	×××　5fr	××　8fr	×××　6fr
2 1 1	1 3 2	3 3 3	2 3 1

Intro　　　　　|B♭　　　|F　　　　|E♭　B♭　|F　　B♭　||

Chorus 1

      B♭　　　　　　　　　|F
      One love,

      　　　　　　|
One heart.
E♭　　　　　B♭　　　　|F　　　B♭
Let's get to - gether and feel alright.
      　　　　　　|
Hear the children crying, (One love.)
      　　　　　|F
Hear the children crying. (One heart.)
      　　|E♭　　　　　　B♭
Saying, give thanks and praise to the Lord
      |F　　　B♭
And I will feel alright.
      |E♭　　　B♭　　　|F　　B♭
Saying, let's get to - gether and feel alright.
      　　　　　　||
Whoa, whoa, whoa, whoa.

Verse 1

      B♭   **Gm**   **|E♭**
     Let them all pass all their

          B♭
Dirty re - marks.

      | **Gm**
(One love.) There is one question

   |E♭   **B♭**
I'd really love to ask.

     | **Gm**   **|E♭**
(One heart.)Is there a place for the

          B♭
Hopeless sin - ner

       | **Gm**   **|E♭**
Who has hurt all man - kind just to

F   **B♭**   **‖**
Save his own? Believe me.

Chorus 2

B♭   **|F**
     One love, what about a one heart? (One heart.)

      |E♭   **B♭**   **|F**   **B♭**
What about, let's get to - gether and feel alright.

             |
As it was in the be - ginning. (One love.)

        |F
So shall it be in the end. (One heart.)

   |E♭   **B♭**
Give thanks and praise to the Lord,

     |F   **B♭**   **|**
And I will feel alright,

E♭   **B♭**   **|F**   **B♭**
Let's a get to - gether and feel alright.

          ‖
One more thing.

Verse 2

B♭   **Gm**
    Let's get to - gether
    |**E♭**   **B♭**
To fight this holy Arma - geddon.
    | **Gm**
(One love.) So when the man come
    |**E♭** **F**   **B♭**
There will be no, no doom.
    | **Gm**
(One soul.) Have pity on those
    |**E♭**   **B♭**
Whose chances grow thinner.
    | **Gm**
There ain't no hiding place
    |**E♭** **F** **B♭**
From the Father of Crea - tion.

Chorus 3

   ‖
Saying,
B♭ |**F**
    One love, what about a one heart? (One heart.)
    |**E♭**   **B♭** |**F**   **B♭**
What about, let's get to - gether and feel alright.
    | |**F**
I'm pleading to mankind, (One love.) whoa.
    |**E♭**   **B♭**
(One heart,) Give thanks and praise to the Lord
    |**F**   **B♭** |
And I will feel alright.
E♭   **B♭** |**F**   **B♭**
Let's get to - gether and feel alright.
  |**E♭**   **B♭** |**F**   **B♭**
Give thanks and praise to the Lord, and I will feel alright,
  |**E♭**   **B♭** |**F**   **B♭** ‖
So, let's get to - gether and feel alright.

Redemption Song

Words and Music by Bob Marley

G   C   D   Em   G/B   Am   Am6

Intro

|G |C   D |G |C   D   G |

| |C   D |G |C   D   G

Verse 1

    ‖**G** |**Em**
Old pirates, yes, they rob I,
   |**C**   **G/B** |**Am** |**G**
Sold I to the merchant ships
                |**Em** |**C**
Minutes after they took I
       G/B |**Am**
From the bottomless pit.
    |**G** |**Em** |**C**
But my hand was made strong
       G/B |**Am**
By the hand of The Almight - y.
    |**G** |**Em** |**C**
We for - ward in this gener - ation
       |**D** |
Triumphant - ly.

Chorus 1

           ‖**G** |**C**
Won't you help to sing
   D |**G**
These songs of freedom?
    |**C**   **D** |**Em** |**C**
'Cause all I ever have,
   D |**G** |**C**
Re - demption songs,
   D |**G** |**C**   **D**
Re - demption songs.

Verse 2

```
 ‖G                              |Em
Emanci - pate yourselves from mental slavery,
        |C          G/B     |Am
None but our - selves can free our minds.
        |G                   |Em
Have no fear for atomic en - ergy,
        |C          G/B     |D
'Cause none of them can stop the time.
        |G                   |Em
How long shall they kill our proph - ets
        |C          G/B        |Am
While we stand aside and look?
        |G          |Em
Oo, some say it's just a part of it.
        |C       G/B    |D          |
We've got to ful - fill the book.
```

Chorus 2

```
                        ‖G           |C
Won't you help to sing
     D        |G
These songs of freedom?
        |C    D    |Em          |C
'Cause all I ever had,
     D        |G          |C
Re - demption songs,
     D        |G          |C
Re - demption songs,
     D        |G          |C    D    |
Re - demption songs.
```

Interlude

```
|Em          |C    D    |Em          |C    D    |
|Em          |C    D    |Em          |C    D
```

Verse 3

```
            ‖G                          |Em
Emanci - pate yourselves from mental slavery,
            |C          G/B       |Am
None but our - selves can free our mind.
            |G                          |Em
Whoa, have no fear for atomic en - ergy,
            |C          G/B       |D
'Cause none of them can stop the time.
            |G                          |Em
How long shall they kill our proph - ets
            |C          G/B          |Am
While we stand aside and look?
            |G              |Em
Yes, some say it's just a part of it.
            |C         G/B       |D            |
We've got to ful - fill the book.
```

Chorus 3

```
                      ‖G                    |C
Won't you help to sing
       D          |G
These songs of freedom?
       |C    D     |Em          |C
'Cause all I ever had,
       D      |G          |
Re - demption songs.
C    D    |Em          |C
All I ever had,
       D      |Em          |C
Re - demption songs.
       D          |G          |C
These songs of freedom,
D            |G          ‖
Songs of free - dom.
```

Outro

```
|C   G/B   |Am          |            |
|Am6          |            ‖
```

So Much Trouble in the World

Words and Music by Bob Marley

Am   Dm   Em   F   E7   F9   G9

Intro

‖:Am |Dm   Em   :‖

Chorus 1

|Am |Dm |
So much trouble in the world.
|Am |Dm   ‖
So much trouble in the world.

Verse 1

|Am |Dm |Am
    Bless my eyes this morning.
                    |Dm |Am
Jah's sun is on the rise once again.
                            |Dm |Am
The way earthly things are going,
                    |Dm
Anything can happen.

Pre-Chorus 1

                    ‖Am |F   Em |
You see, men sailing on their ego trips.
Am |F   Em
Blast off on their spaceships.
        |Am |F   Em
Million miles from reality,
    |Am |F   Em   ‖
No care for you, no care for me.

Chorus 2

Am |Dm |
So much trouble in the world.
Am   **|Dm**
So much trouble in the world.
                     |Am
All you gotta do is

Give a little, (Give a little,)
                   |Dm
Take a little, (Take a little.)

Give a little,
 |E7   **|Am**
One more time, yeah,

                             |Dm
(Give a little,) Yeah, (take a little,) yeah,
           E7   ‖
(Give a little.) Yeah.

Bridge

F9
  So you think you've found the solution,

But it's just another illusion.
                               |G9
(So before you check out this tide)

Don't leave another cornerstone standing there behind, yeah.

Verse 2

           Am   **|Dm**   **|Am**
                We've got to face the day,

               |Dm   **|Am**
Oo, wee, come what may.

                       |Dm   **|Am**
We, the street people talking,

                 |Dm
Yeah, we the people struggling.

Instrumental   **‖:Am**   **|Dm**   **Em**   **:‖**

Pre-Chorus 2

                ‖Am |
Now they're sitting on the time bomb.

   F   **Em** |
(Ba, ba, ba, ba, ba, ba.)

Am |
Now I know the time has come.

   F   **Em**
(Ba, ba, ba, ba, ba, ba.)

     |Am |
What goes on up is coming on down.

   F   **Em** |
(Ba, ba, ba, ba, ba, ba.)

Am |
Goes around and comes around.

   F   **Em**   **‖**
(Ba, ba, ba, ba, ba.)

Outro-Chorus   *Repeat Chorus 1*

Satisfy My Soul

Words and Music by Bob Marley

G   Bm   Am   D   C

Intro

|G |Bm |Am |D |

|G |Bm |Am |D

Verse 1

‖G
Oh, please,

    |Bm
Don't you rock

 |Am |D
My boat. (Don't rock my boat.)

    |G
'Cause I don't

  |Bm
Want my boat

  |Am |D
To be rocking. (Don't rock my boat.)

Verse 2   *Repeat Verse 1*

Pre-Chorus 1

       ‖C |
I'm telling you that, oh,

     |
Oh, wah, whoa, wah, whoa,

| |D
I like it, like it like this.

| | |
So keep my soul laugh - ing.

    |C |
And you should know,

      |
You should know by now,

| |D
I like it,

  | |
I like it like this.

     | ‖
I like it like this, oo, yeah.

Chorus 1

|Am |

                  |D |
You satis - fy my soul, yeah.
                    |Am |
Whoa, yeah.
                  |D |
You satis - fy my soul.
                  |Am |
Every little action
            |D |
Is a re - action.
                  |C
Oh, can't you see

  |
What you've done
  |G
For me,

  |
Oh, yeah.
                  |C |
I'm happy in - side,
D |G
All, all of the time,
  | ‖
Oh,

Verse 3

Am |

            |D | |Am
When we (Bend.) bend - a new corners,
  | |D | |Am
I feel like a (Sweep.) sweepstake winner.
      | |D |
When I meet you around the corner, (Around the corner.)
            |Am |
You make me feel like
                  |D
A sweepstakes winner.
      | ‖
Whoa, child.

Pre-Chorus 2

C | |
 Can't you see,

    | |D
You must be - lieve me?

    | |
Oh, dar - ling, darling,

    | |C
I'm call - ing, calling.

    | |
Can't you see,

    | |D
Why won't you believe me?

    | |
Oh, darling, darling,

    | ‖
I'm call - ing, I'm calling.

Verse 4

Am | |D |
 When I meet you around the corner,

  |Am
Oh, I said, baby,

 | |D |
Nev - er let me be a loner.

   |Am |
And then you hold me tight,

   |D |
You make me feel alright.

   |Am |
Yes, when you hold me tight,

   |D |
You make me feel alright,

   ‖
Woman.

Pre-Chorus 3

C | |
  Can't you see,

      | |D
Won't you be - lieve me?

     | |
Oh, dar - ling, darling,

   | |C
I'm calling, calling.

     | |
Can't you see.

      | |D
Why won't you believe me?

   | |
Oh, darling, darling,

   | ‖
I'm calling, calling.

Outro-Chorus

Am | |D
   Satisfy my soul,

  | |Am
Satisfy my soul.

  | |D
Satisfy my soul,

  | |Am
Satisfy my soul.

   | |D
That's all I want to do,

   | |Am
That's all I'll take from you.

  | |D
Satisfy my soul,

  | ‖
Satisfy my soul.

from *One Love: The Very Best of Bob Marley and the Wailers*

Three Little Birds

Words and Music by Bob Marley

A   D   E

Intro |A | | |

Chorus 1

‖A
Don't worry

|
About a thing,

|D |A
'Cause every little thing gonna be alright.

|
Singin', "Don't worry

|
About a thing,

|D |A
'Cause every little thing gonna be alright."

Verse 1

‖A
Rise up this morning,

|E
Smile with the rising sun.

|A
Three little birds

|D
Pitched by my doorstep,

|A
Singin' sweet songs

|E
Of melodies pure and true

|D |A
Sayin',   "This is my message to you, woo, hoo."

	‖**A**
Chorus 2	Singin', "Don't worry

Chorus 2

‖**A**
Singin', "Don't worry

|
About a thing,

|**D** |**A**
'Cause every little thing is gonna be alright."

|
Singin', "Don't worry, don't worry

|
About a thing,

|**D** |**A**
'Cause every little thing gonna be alright."

Verse 2   *Repeat Verse 1*

Outro-Chorus

‖**A**
Singin', "Don't worry

|
About a thing,

|
Worry about a thing, no.

D |**A**
Every little thing gonna be alright."

|
Don't worry, singin', "Don't worry

|
About a thing,

|**D** |**A**
I won't worry, 'cause every little thing gonna be alright."

|
Hmm, don't worry

|
About a thing,

|**D** |**A**
'Cause, uh, every little thing is gonna be alright.

|
I won't worry, baby, don't worry

|
About a thing,

|**D** |**A**
'Cause every little thing is gonna be alright.

|
Baby, don't worry

|
About a thing, no girl,

|**D**   ‖
'Cause every little thing is gonna be alright.

Stir It Up

Words and Music by Bob Marley

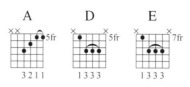

Intro   ‖: A |D   E   :‖ *Play 4 times*

Chorus 1

        A |**D**
Stir it up,

           E |**A**
Little darling, stir it up.

                |D   **E**
Come on, ba - by.

             |A   **|D**
Come on and stir it up,

        E |
Little darling,

A |**D**   **E**
Stir it up, oh.

Verse 1

            ‖A   **|D**
It's been a long, long time

        E   **|A**   **|D**   **E**
Since I've got you on my mind, (Oo.) oh.

    |A   **|D**   **E**
And now you are here, I say it's so clear

    |A   **|D**
To see what a - we will do, baby,

        E
Just me and you.

Chorus 2

```
                   ‖A
Come on and stir it up,
                 |D
I wanna say,
        E
Little darling.
      |A
Yeah, stir it up.
                 |D       E
Come on, ba - by.
                 |A               |D
Come on and stir it up, yeah,
        E            |
Little darling.
A                |D      E     ‖
Stir it up, whoa.
```

Verse 2

```
A                          |D
I'll push the wood and I'll
        E       |A
Blaze your fire.

                      |D
Then I'll satisfy your...
              E      |A
Heart's de - sire.
                     |D
Said, I stir it, yeah,
        E         |A
Every minute.

                      |D
All you've got to do, baby,
        E            ‖
Is keep it in and...
```

Chorus 3

```
A                    |D
Stir it up, come on,
        E         |
Little darling.
A
Stir it up.
              |D      E
I'm already thirsty.
                 |A               |D
Come on and stir it up, oh, oh,
        E         |
Little darling.
A
Stir it up,
    |D        E
Whoa, mm.
```

Verse 3

             ‖**A** |**D**
And then   quench me

                    E |**A**
When I'm thirst - y.

                            |**D**
Come on, cool me down, ba - by,

  E |**A**
When I'm hot.

                  |**D**
Your recipe, darling,

  E |**A**
Is so tasty.

              |**D**
And you sure

        E   ‖
Can stir your pot, so...

Outro-Chorus

A |**D**
Stir it up, oh,

    E |**A**
Little darling, stir it up.

 |**D**   **E**
Oh, yeah.

             |**A** |**D**
Come on and stir it up, oh,

    E |
Little darling.

A |**D**
Stir it up, yeah.

     E |
Come on, come on and

A |**D**
Stir it up, whoa,

    E |
Little darling.

A   ‖
Stir it up.

from *One Love: The Very Best of Bob Marley and the Wailers*

Turn Your Lights Down Low

Words and Music by Bob Marley

C6/D   D   G   D/F#   Em   C   Bm7   Am7   D7sus4   Cmaj7   D*

Intro

|C6/D D |C6/D D ‖

Verse 1

G   D/F#   Em | |C
Turn your lights down low

Bm7   Am7 | D7sus4 |G
And pull your win - dow curtains.

D/F#   Em | |
Oh, let Jah moon come shin - ing in,

Cmaj7 Bm7 Am7 | C6/D
Into our life a - gain,

Pre-Chorus 1

D ‖Cmaj7   Bm7
Sayin', oo,

Am7 | Bm7 |Cmaj7
It's been a long, long time.

Bm7   Am7 | Bm7 |Cmaj7
I kept this message for you, girl,

Bm7   Am7| Bm7 |Cmaj7
But it seems I was never on time.

Bm7   Am7 |
Still I want to get through to you, girl - ie,

|C6/D D
On   time,

|C6/D D   ‖
On   time.

Chorus 1

        G   **D/F♯**   **Em** |
     I want to give you some love.

               D* |**C**
(Good, good lovin'.)

           Bm7   **Am7**|
I want to give you some good,   good lovin'.

 D7sus4
(Good, good lovin'.)

 |**G**
Oh I,

 D/F♯   **Em** |
Oh I,

           |**C**
Oh, I.

          Bm7   **Am7**|
Say, I want to give you some good,   good lovin'.

                   ‖
(Good, good lovin'.)

Verse 2

    G   **D/F♯**   **Em** | |**Cmaj7**
   Turn your lights down low.

           Bm7   **Am7**|
Never, never try to re - sist,

             |**G**
Oh, no.

     D/F♯ |**Em** |
Oh, let my love come tum - bling in,

Cmaj7 **Bm7** **Am7** |
Into our life a - gain,

Pre-Chorus 2

       Bm7‖**Cmaj7**   **Bm7**
Say - in',   oo,

  Am7| **Bm7** |**Cmaj7**
I love ya.

      Bm7   **Am7**| **Bm7**
And I want you to know right now,

     |**Cmaj7**   **Bm7**
(Oo, oo.) Oo. (Oo.)

 Am7| **Bm7** |**Cmaj7**
I love ya.

      Bm7   **Am7**|
And I want you to know right now.

    |**C6/D** **D**
'Cause I,

    |**C6/D** **D**   ‖
'Cause I...

Chorus 2

G   **D/F♯**   **Em** | **D*** |**C**
  I want to give you some love,   oh,

      Bm7   **Am7**|
I want to give you some good,   good lovin'.

   |**G**   **D/F♯**   **Em** | |**C**
Oh, I,   I want to give you some love,   say,

     Bm7   **Am7**| **C6/D** **D** ‖
I want to give you some good,   good lovin'.

Outro

G   **D/F♯**   **Em** |
  Turn your lights down low,

       |**Cmaj7**
Whoa.

      Bm7   **Am7** |
Never, never try to resist,

Oh, no.

   |**G**   **D/F♯**   **Em**| |
Oo, let my love, oh, let my love come tumbling in,

Cmaj7 **Bm7**   **Am7**|
Into   our life a - gain,

    |**G**
Oh.

     D/F♯   **Em**   ‖
I want to give you some love.

Waiting in Vain

Words and Music by Bob Marley

A♭maj7 D♭maj7 D♭ E♭ Cm B♭m

Intro

|A♭maj7 |D♭maj7 |A♭maj7 |D♭maj7 |

‖:A♭maj7 |D♭maj7   :‖
I don't wanna wait in vain for your love.

Verse 1

A♭maj7 |D♭maj7 |A♭maj7
From the very first time I placed my eyes on you, girl,
|D♭maj7 |A♭maj7
My heart says follow through.
|D♭maj7 |A♭maj7
But I know now that I'm way down on your line,
|D♭maj7 |A♭maj7
But the waiting feel is fine.
|D♭maj7 |A♭maj7
So don't treat me like a puppet on a string,
|D♭maj7 |A♭maj7
'Cause I know how to my thing.
|D♭maj7 |A♭maj7
Don't talk to me as if you think I'm dumb,
|D♭maj7
I wanna know when you're gonna come.

Chorus 1

‖A♭maj7 |D♭maj7 |
See, I don't wanna wait in vain for your love.
A♭maj7 |D♭maj7 |
I don't wanna wait in vain for your love.
A♭maj7 |D♭maj7 |D♭
I don't wanna wait in vain for your love, 'cause if
E♭ |
Sum - mer is here,
Cm   B♭m |D♭
I'm still wait - ing there.
E♭ |Cm   B♭m   ‖
Winter is here and I'm still wait - ing there.

Guitar Solo ‖: A♭maj7 |D♭maj7 |A♭maj7 |D♭maj7   :‖

Verse 2

‖A♭maj7
Like I said,

      |D♭maj7
It's been three years since I'm

     |A♭maj7
Knocking on your door

      |D♭maj7
And I can still knock some more.

 |A♭maj7 |D♭maj7
Oo, girl, oo, girl, is it feasible,

      |A♭maj7
I want to know now,

     |D♭maj7
For I to knock some more?

  |A♭maj7
Ya see,

    |D♭maj7
In life I know

     |A♭maj7
There's lots of grief,

     |D♭maj7
But your love is my re - lief.

 |A♭maj7 |D♭maj7
Tears in my eyes burn, tears in my eyes burn.

  |A♭maj7 |D♭maj7
While I'm waiting, while I'm waiting for my turn.

Outro-Chorus

‖A♭maj7 |D♭maj7 |
See, I don't wanna wait in vain for your love.

A♭maj7 |D♭maj7 |
I don't wanna wait in vain for your love.

A♭maj7 |D♭maj7 |
I don't wanna wait in vain for your love.

A♭maj7 |D♭maj7 |
I don't wanna wait in vain for your love.

A♭maj7 |D♭maj7 |
I don't wanna wait in vain for your love, whoa.

A♭maj7
I don't wanna, I don't wanna, I don't wanna,

         |D♭maj7
I don't wanna, I don't wanna wait in vain.

  |A♭maj7
No, I don't wanna, I don't wanna, I don't wanna,

         |D♭maj7 |
I don't wanna, I don't wanna wait in vain, no.

‖:A♭maj7
  (I don't wanna, I don't wanna, I don't wanna,

         |D♭maj7   :‖ *Repeat and fade*
I don't wanna, I don't wanna wait in vain.)

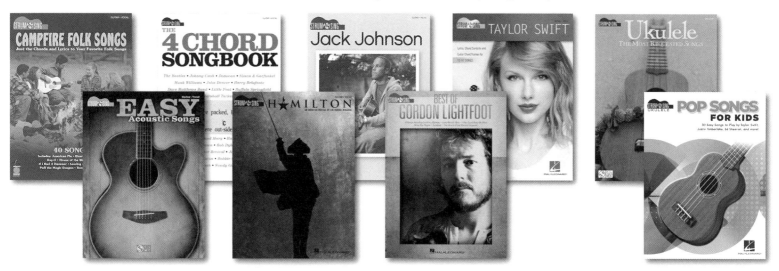

STRUM & SING

The Strum & Sing series for guitar and ukulele provides an unplugged and pared-down approach to your favorite songs – just the chords and the lyrics, with nothing fancy. These easy-to-play arrangements are designed for both aspiring and professional musicians.

GUITAR

Acoustic Classics
00191891 ....$15.99

Adele
00159855 ....$12.99

Sara Bareilles
00102354 ....$12.99

The Beatles
00172234 ....$17.99

Blues
00159335 ....$12.99

Zac Brown Band
02501620 ....$19.99

Colbie Caillat
02501725 ....$14.99

Campfire Folk Songs
02500686 ....$15.99

Chart Hits of 2014-2015
00142554 ....$12.99

Chart Hits of 2015-2016
00156248 ....$12.99

Best of Kenny Chesney
00142457 ....$14.99

Christmas Carols
00348351 ....$14.99

Christmas Songs
00171332 ....$14.99

Kelly Clarkson
00146384 ....$14.99

Coffeehouse Songs for Guitar
00285991 ....$14.99

Leonard Cohen
00265489 ....$14.99

Dear Evan Hansen
00295108 ....$16.99

John Denver Collection
02500632 ....$17.99

Disney
00233900 ....$17.99

Eagles
00157994 ....$14.99

Easy Acoustic Songs
00125478 ....$19.99

Billie Eilish
00363094 ....$14.99

The Five-Chord Songbook
02501718 ....$14.99

Folk Rock Favorites
02501669 ....$14.99

Folk Songs
02501482 ....$14.99

The Four-Chord Country Songbook
00114936 ....$15.99

The Four Chord Songbook
02501533 ....$14.99

Four Chord Songs
00249581 ....$16.99

The Greatest Showman
00278383 ....$14.99

Hamilton
00217116 ....$15.99

Jack Johnson
02500858 ....$19.99

Robert Johnson
00191890 ....$12.99

Carole King
00115243 ....$10.99

Best of Gordon Lightfoot
00139393 ....$15.99

Dave Matthews Band
02501078 ....$10.95

John Mayer
02501636 ....$19.99

The Most Requested Songs
02501748 ....$16.99

Jason Mraz
02501452 ....$14.99

**Tom Petty –
Wildflowers & All the Rest**
00362682 ....$14.99

Elvis Presley
00198890 ....$12.99

Queen
00218578 ....$12.99

Rock Around the Clock
00103625 ....$12.99

Rock Ballads
02500872 ....$9.95

Rocketman
00300469 ....$17.99

Ed Sheeran
00152016 ....$14.99

The Six-Chord Songbook
02502277 ....$17.99

Chris Stapleton
00362625 ....$19.99

Cat Stevens
00116827 ....$17.99

Taylor Swift
00159856 ....$14.99

The Three-Chord Songbook
00211634 ....$12.99

Top Christian Hits
00156331 ....$12.99

Top Hits of 2016
00194288 ....$12.99

Keith Urban
00118558 ....$14.99

The Who
00103667 ....$12.99

Yesterday
00301629 ....$14.99

Neil Young – Greatest Hits
00138270 ....$15.99

UKULELE

The Beatles
00233899 ....$16.99

Colbie Caillat
02501731 ....$10.99

Coffeehouse Songs
00138238 ....$14.99

John Denver
02501694 ....$17.99

The 4-Chord Ukulele Songbook
00114331 ....$16.99

Jack Johnson
02501702 ....$19.99

John Mayer
02501706 ....$10.99

The Most Requested Songs
02501453 ....$15.99

Jason Mraz
02501753 ....$14.99

Pop Songs for Kids
00284415 ....$16.99

Sing-Along Songs
02501710 ....$16.99

HAL•LEONARD®

halleonard.com
Visit our website to see full song lists
or order from your favorite retailer.

Get Better at Guitar
...with these Great Guitar Instruction Books from Hal Leonard!

101 GUITAR TIPS
INCLUDES TAB
STUFF ALL THE PROS KNOW AND USE
by Adam St. James
This book contains invaluable guidance on everything from scales and music theory to truss rod adjustments, proper recording studio set-ups, and much more.
00695737 Book/Online Audio $17.99

AMAZING PHRASING
INCLUDES TAB
by Tom Kolb
This book/audio pack explores all the main components necessary for crafting well-balanced rhythmic and melodic phrases. It also explains how these phrases are put together to form cohesive solos. The companion audio contains 89 demo tracks, most with full-band backing.
00695583 Book/Online Audio $22.99

ARPEGGIOS FOR THE MODERN GUITARIST
INCLUDES TAB
by Tom Kolb
Using this no-nonsense book with online audio, guitarists will learn to apply and execute all types of arpeggio forms using a variety of techniques, including alternate picking, sweep picking, tapping, string skipping, and legato.
00695862 Book/Online Audio $22.99

BLUES YOU CAN USE
by John Ganapes
This comprehensive source for learning blues guitar is designed to develop both your lead and rhythm playing. Includes: 21 complete solos • blues chords, progressions and riffs • turnarounds • movable scales and soloing techniques • string bending • utilizing the entire fingerboard • and more.
00142420 Book/Online Media.................................$22.99

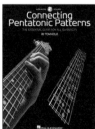

CONNECTING PENTATONIC PATTERNS
INCLUDES TAB
by Tom Kolb
If you've been finding yourself trapped in the pentatonic box, this book is for you! This hands-on book with online audio offers examples for guitar players of all levels, from beginner to advanced. Study this book faithfully, and soon you'll be soloing all over the neck with the greatest of ease.
00696445 Book/Online Audio $24.99

FRETBOARD MASTERY
INCLUDES TAB
by Troy Stetina
Untangle the mysterious regions of the guitar fretboard and unlock your potential. This book familiarizes you with all the shapes you need to know by applying them in real musical examples, thereby reinforcing and reaffirming your newfound knowledge.
00695331 Book/Online Audio $22.99

GUITAR AEROBICS
INCLUDES TAB
by Troy Nelson
Here is a daily dose of guitar "vitamins" to keep your chops fine tuned! Musical styles include rock, blues, jazz, metal, country, and funk. Techniques taught include alternate picking, arpeggios, sweep picking, string skipping, legato, string bending, and rhythm guitar.
00695946 Book/Online Audio $24.99

GUITAR CLUES
INCLUDES TAB
OPERATION PENTATONIC
by Greg Koch
Whether you're new to improvising or have been doing it for a while, this book/audio pack will provide loads of delicious licks and tricks that you can use right away, from volume swells and chicken pickin' to intervallic and chordal ideas.
00695827 Book/Online Audio $19.99

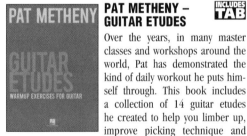

PAT METHENY – GUITAR ETUDES
INCLUDES TAB
Over the years, in many master classes and workshops around the world, Pat has demonstrated the kind of daily workout he puts himself through. This book includes a collection of 14 guitar etudes he created to help you limber up, improve picking technique and build finger independence.
00696587.................................$17.99

PICTURE CHORD ENCYCLOPEDIA
This comprehensive guitar chord resource for all playing styles and levels features five voicings of 44 chord qualities for all twelve keys – 2,640 chords in all! For each, there is a clearly illustrated chord frame, as well as *an actual photo* of the chord being played!.
00695224.................................$22.99

RHYTHM GUITAR 365
INCLUDES TAB
by Troy Nelson
This book provides 365 exercises – one for every day of the year! – to keep your rhythm chops fine tuned. Topics covered include: chord theory; the fundamentals of rhythm; fingerpicking; strum patterns; diatonic and non-diatonic progressions; triads; major and minor keys; and more.
00103627 Book/Online Audio $27.99

SCALE CHORD RELATIONSHIPS
INCLUDES TAB
by Michael Mueller & Jeff Schroedl
This book/audio pack explains how to: recognize keys • analyze chord progressions • use the modes • play over nondiatonic harmony • use harmonic and melodic minor scales • use symmetrical scales • incorporate exotic scales • and much more!
00695563 Book/Online Audio $17.99

SPEED MECHANICS FOR LEAD GUITAR
INCLUDES TAB
by Troy Stetina
Take your playing to the stratosphere with this advanced lead book which will help you develop speed and precision in today's explosive playing styles. Learn the fastest ways to achieve speed and control, secrets to make your practice time really count, and how to open your ears and make your musical ideas more solid and tangible.
00699323 Book/Online Audio $22.99

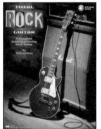

TOTAL ROCK GUITAR
INCLUDES TAB
by Troy Stetina
This comprehensive source for learning rock guitar is designed to develop both your lead and rhythm playing. It covers: getting a tone that rocks • open chords, power chords and barre chords • riffs, scales and licks • string bending, strumming, and harmonics • and more.
00695246 Book/Online Audio $22.99

Guitar World Presents
STEVE VAI'S GUITAR WORKOUT
INCLUDES TAB
In this book, Steve Vai reveals his path to virtuoso enlightenment with two challenging guitar workouts – one 10-hour and one 30-hour – which include scale and chord exercises, ear training, sight-reading, music theory, and much more.
00119643.................................$16.99